EMERGENCY!

EMERGENCY!

BY JOY MASOFF

PRINCIPAL PHOTOGRAPHY BY
BRIAN MICHAUD AND PETER ESCOBEDO

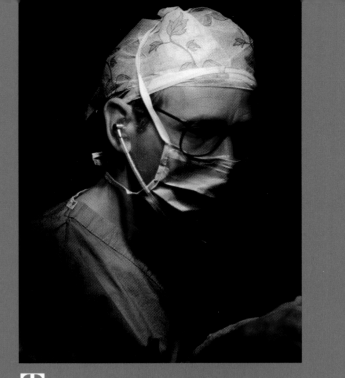

This book is dedicated to every man, woman, or child who has ever answered the cry of a person in need.

Library of Congress Cataloging-in-Publication Data

Masoff, Joy
  Emergency! / by Joy Masoff.
    p. cm.
Summary: Discusses all aspects of emergency medicine including the medical personnel and equipment needed to successfully help the patient.

  ISBN 0-590-97898-5(hc)
  1. Emergency medicine–Juvenile literature. (1. Emergency medicine.) I. Title.
RC86.M37 1998   97-26995
616.02'5--dc21   CIP
                                           AC

10 9 8 7 6 5 4 3 2 1   9/9 0/0 01 02 03

Printed in Mexico 49
First printing, February 1999

A MESSAGE FROM THE EMERGENCY ROOM

WHEN THINGS GO WRONG

HELP IS ON THE WAY

EMERGENCY!

HELP IS HERE

MEDICINE: PAST & FUTURE

START NOW

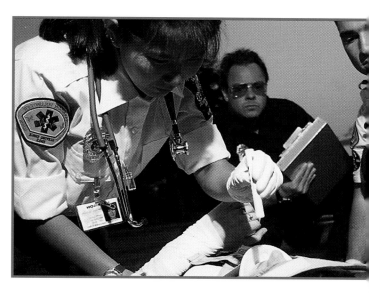

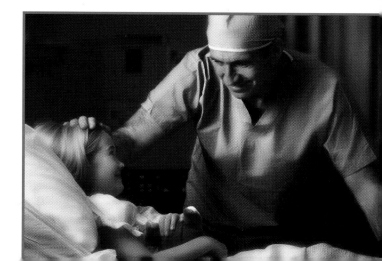

The Magic of

I have been practicing emergency medicine for many years now, both as an emergency room doctor in a busy hospital and as an active volunteer with the ambulance corps in my small town. It's an exciting life, and very hard work. It takes constant training to give the best possible care. Nights *aren't* always for sleeping. Holidays *aren't* always for celebrating. Meals get eaten on the run. But when someone who has been hurt or is ill says "You saved my life," all the exhaustion disappears. There's no better feeling.

Emergency medicine as we know it now hasn't been around very long. Before 1967 there was no 911 to call. There were no medically trained emergency medical technicians (EMTs) to save lives on the go. There were no high-tech trauma centers, ready to treat people with multiple injuries. Now, there are hundreds of trauma centers, over 4,850 emergency rooms, and close to 17,000 fully staffed ambulances in the United States alone. Well over a half million people are certified EMTs.

Car accidents, sports injuries, and heart attacks still happen. Some babies are born too soon, and elderly people still break bones all too easily. But now, something can be done. Dial 911 and within minutes a team of trained professionals will be on the way, ready to swiftly and safely stabilize and move a patient to the hospital. And the team that waits in the emergency room, having been briefed by the ambulance crew, will be waiting to do everything they can to set that patient on the road to recovery.

Emergency Medicine

The human body is like an enormous jigsaw puzzle with a million little pieces. The job of the emergency room staff is to figure out which of those pieces is not fitting right. Now, putting a puzzle together takes time and patience, but emergency medical workers often find time is in short supply.

Fortunately, we have help. We turn to tools like X rays, CAT scans, and machines that graph how the heart is working. We study the results of blood and fluid tests. We have a patient's history—everything the patient and the patient's family can tell us. Using these and our own observations, we quickly figure out what's wrong. And while high-tech tools are a great help, our eyes and ears…looking at the patient and listening carefully to what his or her body is saying…often works the best.

Every day there are new discoveries that help us learn more about the human body. Yet, the more we learn, the more we marvel at the body's many mysteries. To watch a stopped heart start beating again…to see a patient who was near death laughing with his friends…these are the moments we all live for.

Jill Slater Waldman, MD
Clinical Professor, Emergency Medicine at Cornell University Medical College.
Attending Physician in Emergency Medicine,
United Hospital Medical Center, Port Chester, NY.
Active member, Lewisboro Volunteer Ambulance Corps, South Salem, NY.

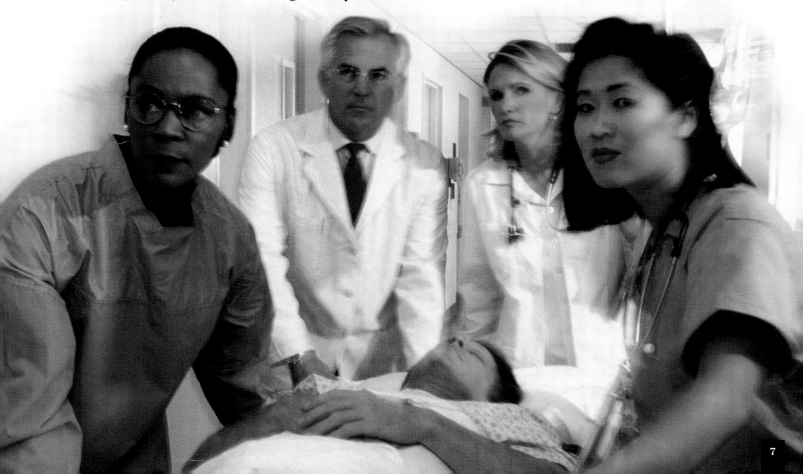

It all happens so quickly. One minute you're fine, riding your bike or munching on a tuna sandwich. But in one split second, all that changes. Your bike hits a crack in the road and you go flying over the handlebars. Or that tuna salad turns your stomach into a hot ball of pain. You are in trouble. Your body needs help.

We Have an Emergency!

There are 206 bones in your body…501 different skeletal muscles…a heart that pumps 450 million pints of blood in a lifetime…miles of veins and arteries woven throughout. When things are going right, every part works in perfect harmony with the next. But when things go wrong—and they can go wrong in a split second—help is needed. And it's needed fast.

IN THE BLINK OF AN EYE…

An accident has just happened. A midfield collision during a ball game has left one player lying motionless on the field. A crowd gathers, unable to do anything but worry. The coach kneels at the side of the player, trying, with trembling fingers, to feel the soft rhythm of a PULSE, a sign that the heart is still moving blood through the body. The injured player needs help, but everyone feels helpless. What can they do? Where do they even begin?

Emergencies remind us just how quickly things change, from healthy to unwell in the time it takes to snap your fingers. But almost as quickly as the trouble begins, there are people waiting to help— paramedics, doctors, and nurses, who can fix what's broken, search out deadly bacteria, and make the hurt go away.

AIR GOES IN AND OUT.
BLOOD GOES ROUND AND ROUND.
ANY VARIATION ON THAT IS A BAD THING.

When EMERGENCY MEDICAL TECHNICIANS, also called EMTs, begin their training, their teachers sometimes jokingly share that simple lesson with them. But as simple as it sounds, it sums up the challenges every medical worker faces.

Our bodies have two enemies—INJURY and ILLNESS. Injuries happen from the outside, when the skin that protects our bodies is cut open, or when the muscles, ligaments, tendons, and bones that support our organs are damaged by a sudden impact. A deep cut will allow too much blood to escape and too many germs to creep in. Broken bones and torn ligaments will not support our weight. They must be fixed.

Illnesses develop on the inside. Bacteria, viruses, and parasites invade our bodies' protective shields and upset the perfect balance of our systems. Some germs are as easy to spot as a broken bone or sprained ankle. Some invaders hide so well, they are almost impossible to find.

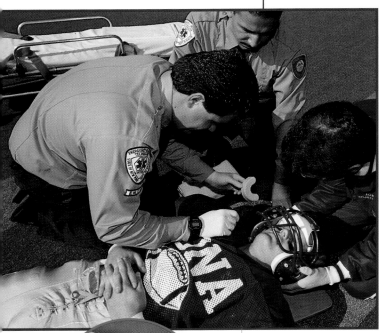

The enemies up close. A microscope unmasks strands of sickness in a deadly strep bacteria (above) and a flu virus (right).

SMALL BUT DANGEROUS

Illnesses fall into two categories. ACUTE illnesses come on suddenly, with little warning. Most turn out to be nothing more than a bad cold or sore throat, but some are life threatening. A knifelike pain behind the belly button that just won't quit, a fever that climbs above 104° Fahrenheit…these are signs of illnesses that need medical attention immediately. CHRONIC illnesses never really go away. A person with asthma, for example, has a chronic condition that may have to be managed for years.

GET HELP…FAST!

Sometimes the signs of danger aren't so obvious. A bit of heartburn after a spicy lunch, a headache that just won't go away…these can be just as dangerous as the messiest car crash. A newborn baby with a slight fever might be in serious trouble, and a toddler who swallows a whole bottle of medicine can put brain, heart, and lungs in grave danger. These people all need help, and they need it NOW.

CALL 911

Three easy-to-remember numbers. Thousands of amazing rescues. Since the 911 network was started in 1967, it has helped over a million people. Young children have saved mothers who were hurt. Alert neighbors have become next-door heroes.

The DISPATCHERS who answer the calls are the first in a long line of men and women devoted to saving lives. They have a hard job to do. One misunderstood word can cost a life, so 911 operators have to listen very carefully. That can be difficult, since the callers are sometimes upset. Dispatchers answer about 40 calls a day and have only a minute or two to figure out what's wrong. It is their job to figure out if just an ambulance is enough or if more help is needed.

THE CURSE OF 911

Unfortunately, too many people call 911 when they shouldn't. According to one source, only 30% of the calls that come in to 911 are true emergencies. People have called to find out the best temperature to roast a turkey, to complain about noisy neighbors, and just to have a little prankish "fun."

The result? A lot of urgent calls that couldn't get through, and a lot of wasted time spent responding to calls that never should have been made. Never call 911 unless it is *really* an emergency.

YOU CAN BE A LIFESAVER

How can you help if you find yourself with someone who is very ill or has been in an accident? First call 911. Then remember the word AMPLE. If the victim can talk, ask the following questions.

A IS FOR ALLERGIES—Is the person allergic to anything, such as bee stings?

M IS FOR MEDICATIONS—Is the victim taking any drugs for any reason?

P IS FOR PAST MEDICAL HISTORY—Has the patient had this happen before? Does he or she have heart problems or other ongoing medical conditions?

L IS FOR LAST MEAL—When did the victim last eat? If surgery is needed, it's important to know this.

E IS FOR EVENTS LEADING UP TO THE MOMENT—When and how did it happen?

The answers to these questions can really help the EMTs when they arrive on the scene.

Every successful rescue depends on teamwork, from the first call to 911 to the safe arrival at the hospital.

Quick! Call the

A call has just come in to 911. Two cars have skidded into each other on a wet highway. A rescue crew rushes to the scene, the paramedics race to get the victims to the hospital. They have just a few fast-moving minutes. Too much longer and it may be too late.

People can get sick in the middle of the afternoon or in the darkest hours of the night. Accidents can happen in icy March or sunny July. And because no one knows when illness or injury might strike, the men and women of the EMERGENCY MEDICAL SERVICES (EMS) wait…always ready to come at a moment's notice.

THE GOLDEN HOUR

That's what emergency workers call the time between an accident and a patient's arrival at the hospital. An hour may seem like a long time, but if it's hard to reach the victim, if there is a long distance to travel to the nearest hospital, if the patient is in such bad shape that he or she can't be moved without doing more harm—an hour can seem as fast as a minute.

THE CLOCK HAS STARTED TICKING

The rescue crews arrive at the scene, but before the victims can be helped, they have to be removed from their cars. One car has completely flipped over. It is going to be difficult even to reach the patient.

Rescue workers secure both vehicles and make the area as safe as possible. Unstable cars are braced, doors cut off, and roofs peeled back. While firefighters struggle to stabilize the flipped-over car, paramedics treat the passengers in the other car. The driver can answer the paramedic's questions and doesn't seem to be badly injured, but her daughter tells them that her neck hurts. They place a neck brace around her, in case of an injury to her spine, and gently slide her from the car onto a stiff wooden backboard.

The driver of the car that has overturned is clearly in bad shape. Rescuers can see blood everywhere. The driver doesn't answer when they talk to him. His heartbeat and pulse are weak. Quickly they free him from the wreck, and the EMTs get to work.

Before this young patient can be moved, her neck and back will be braced to keep the spinal cord from being injured by loose bone fragments.

EMTs know that the rougher the weather, the tougher the calls.

Paramedics

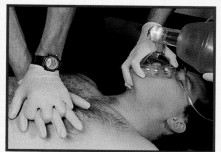

Paramedics and EMTs always remember their ABCs.

A IS FOR AIRWAY—Is there anything blocking the route from the mouth to the lungs? Even a tongue can roll back and keep air from reaching the lungs.

B IS FOR BREATHING—Is the patient able to breathe, or has some damage been done to the lungs?

ALL ABOUT EMERGENCY MEDICAL TECHNICIANS (EMTs)

In very big cities, EMTs are usually part of the fire or police department or linked with a hospital. In smaller towns, rescue crews are devoted volunteers who generously offer up their time. But one thing is the same. They are all dedicated professionals who care tremendously about their patients. The most highly trained EMTs are called PARAMEDICS. They have mastered more difficult medical skills and can do a lot to help critically ill patients even before they reach the hospital.

THE ENEMY? TIME AND SHOCK

Blood pumping through our bodies feeds our organs and keeps us alive. When that flow is stopped, blood can't reach those important parts. Without blood, all the body's systems start to shut down. The heart won't beat. Lungs won't breathe. A body starts to *stop*. SHOCK has set in. Serious injuries with a lot of bleeding usually bring on shock. This is what has happened to the driver of the flipped-over car. For the EMTs, every erratic heartbeat is a reminder that the golden hour is ticking away.

FIGHTING BACK

A call is made to the nearest hospital for advice. The paramedics must get the victim's blood pressure back up. The patient's AIRWAY is blocked, so oxygen can't get to his lungs. They quickly place a tube into his throat, to open up the blockage. They pour fluids into his body through an INTRAVENOUS (IV) LINE. They might give DRUGS to help the heart pump harder. PRESSURE will be applied to the wounds to stop the flow of blood. A DEFIBRILLATOR might be needed to restart a stopped heart. They carefully SPLINT broken limbs.

C IS FOR CIRCULATION—Is the heart pumping? Is heavy bleeding putting the patient at risk for shock?

An INTRAVENOUS LINE helps replace lost body fluids. Paramedics usually use SALINE, which is basically salt water, but LACTATED RINGER'S SOLUTION, a water, salt, chloride, and sugar combo, is sometimes used when a patient is bleeding really badly and the hospital is some distance away.

CATS HAVE NINE LIVES...

EMTs have nine jobs. Tending to the victim is only a part of their duties.

1- BE PREPARED. No one wants to arrive on the scene without oxygen or bandages on the shelves.

2- RESPOND. Get to the scene safely, yet quickly.

3- MAKE SURE THE SCENE IS SAFE. Is a house in danger of collapsing? Will a car roll away? Before caring for a patient, check for safety.

4- GAIN ACCESS. Sometimes car doors have to be cut away or walls braced before an EMT can reach the victim.

5- FIND OUT WHAT'S WRONG. Look. Listen. Feel. Then provide proper care.

6- REMOVE THE PATIENT. Free, lift, and move the victim without causing any further injury.

7- TRANSFER. Prepare the patient for the move to the ambulance.

8- TRANSPORT. Back into the ambulance for the drive to the hospital. Along the way, carefully watch over the patient. At the hospital, deliver the victim into the care of the emergency room staff along with an accurate description of his or her condition.

9- TERMINATION. Return safely from the run. Clean and restock the ambulance and write up a report of the rescue. Then get ready to do it all again.

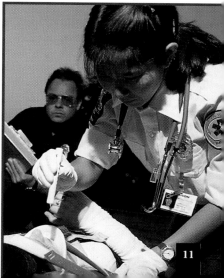

Racing to the Rescue

The call for help has just come in. Fifteen tons of life-saving equipment is roaring on its way. Those ambulances and rescue rigs come packed with hundreds of items. Some are as small as a Band-Aid. Others can lift the heaviest truck. Here's what's inside.

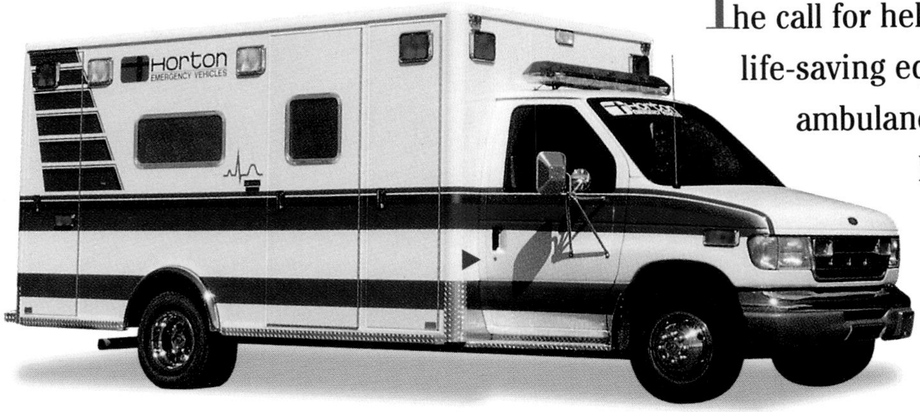

AMBULANCES

Packed to the roof with over 300 items, these compact trucks, which EMTs call RIGS, carry advanced life-care equipment along with a highly trained crew that knows how to use it.

There are three different kinds of ambulance. TYPE I is a truck with a separate cab in the back. TYPE II is a van, with the entire area open. TYPE III (pictured here), which is the kind most big cities use, is the truck type, with a walk-through passage up to the driver's seat.

Advanced Life Support

Medicines to stimulate weak hearts. Fluids to substitute for lost blood. Machines to start stopped hearts.

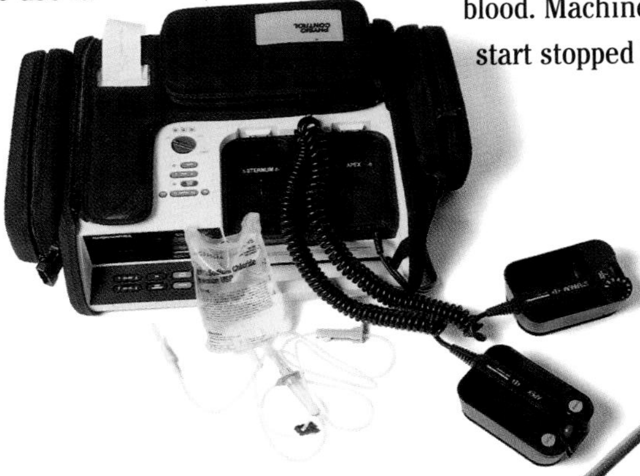

Immobilizers

Broken bones and injured joints need to be kept from moving. Ambulances carry a variety of backboards, braces, and stiff collars to do that job.

Wound Care

Everything from Band-Aids to gauze pads, from elastic bandages to traction splints that brace broken bones.

Stretchers and Stair Chairs

These help rescuers move patients comfortably from the accident scene to the hospital.

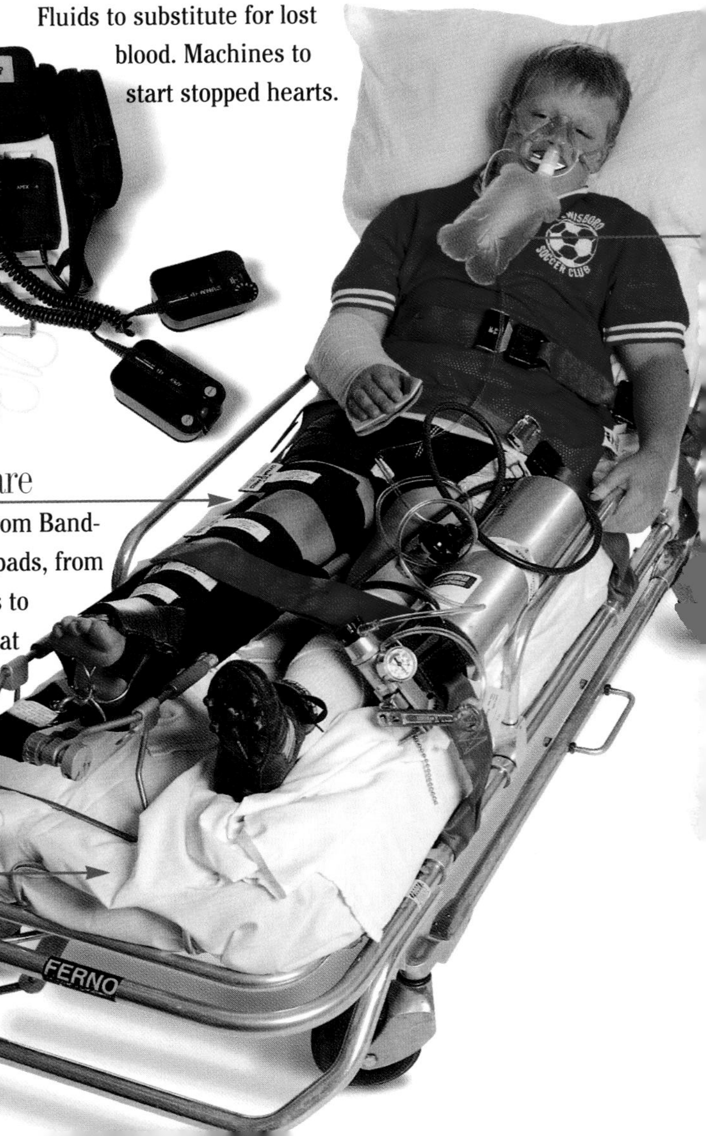

Without the proper gear, a successful rescue is almost impossible. If a building has collapsed, if a train has derailed, if a person has fallen through ice, special equipment is needed. Rescue trucks come packed with all sorts of lifesaving gear.

WHAT'S INSIDE A RESCUE RIG

The best rigs are the ones that can haul the most equipment. Here's what's on board.

◀ POWER TOOLS— such as SPREADERS, CUTTERS, and RAMS that can slice through metal.

◀ INFLATABLE LIFTING BAGS—These are slid under heavy objects, such as a car, and then inflated to lift the heavy object.

▲ TRIPOD—This three-legged stand can be placed over holes and deep shafts so that rescuers can be lowered down.

PERSONAL FLOATATION ▶ DEVICES—For in-water rescues.

ROPES AND CHAINS—For towing and pulling.

SPECIAL STRETCHERS, STOKES LITTERS, or SKEDS—For moving patients from places like caves, swift water, or cliffs.

HIGH-INTENSITY LIGHTS— Necessary for night rescues.

Communicators
Keeping in touch with the hospital and other rescue workers is a must.

Breathing Aids
Oxygen tanks that give patients concentrated O_2 and devices to open up blocked airways.

Personal Protection Gear
Two weights of gloves, face masks, gowns, and more. These keep EMTs from spreading any germs they may have to the patient, as well as protecting the EMTs from any illness the patient may have.

Diagnostic Tools
Stethoscopes, blood-pressure cuffs, pen-lights, otoscopes (for peering at ears and throat), and more.

A Trauma Kit and a Drug Box
Everything EMTs might need for a difficult case all packed in one handy bag. Perfect when they have to get to a hard-to-reach patient. The drug box contains dozens of lifesaving medicines.

A Highly Skilled Crew
Dedicated and devoted to the task of helping those in need.

Sometimes there's no time to get someone to the hospital by ambulance. Sometimes the nearest hospital isn't equipped to handle a particular kind of injury. Sometimes the bleeding is very bad or the patient is very, very sick. That's when rescue workers take to the sky.

We Need Help...Fast!

EMERGENCY ROOMS IN THE AIR

Firefighters have just pulled a person from a burning building. Burn victims need very special care, and the closest hospital does not have a burn unit. A quick decision is made, and a call goes out...a call for a MEDICAL-EVACUATION (MED-EVAC) HELICOPTER.

Within minutes, a chopper (another name for a helicopter) will be on the scene. After loading the patient aboard, the chopper will lift off and swiftly transport the patient to a big hospital, to receive the lifesaving treatment he or she needs to survive and recover.

WHAT'S ON BOARD...

Packed inside the helicopter are the most advanced lifesaving tools there are. There are machines to keep people breathing, or to take over and breathe for them until damaged lungs can be repaired. There are special items for taking care of premature babies (infants that have been born too soon). There are machines that can start a stopped heart. In fact, most of the equipment in the typical emergency room is carried right on board the helicopter.

AND WHO'S ON BOARD

Most copters carry the following crew members:

You can't get off the ground without a PILOT. The people who guide these craft have years and years of flight experience. In New York State for example, each med-evac pilot has over 25 years behind the controls of a plane.

Each crew has a FLIGHT NURSE with many years of critical-care experience. Many are former emergency room nurses who love the thrill of flying. They have been trained to the highest levels, and many have special certification in the care of premature and very ill infants.

Finally, the crew might include a FLIGHT PARAMEDIC, a person who has training in handling people with serious injuries and is an expert in pre-hospital care. You need a whole team to care for a critically ill patient.

READY AND WAITING

On board the helicopter, the nurse is in constant contact with the hospital. If the patient has multiple injuries, a call will go out to alert a whole team of doctors to be ready. The team might include an ORTHOPEDIST to reset broken bones, a SURGEON to operate on a damaged lung, and a NEUROSURGEON to help take care of a head injury, for example. When the helicopter lands, they'll be ready to get to work.

FREQUENT FLIERS

Premature babies are frequently moved from small rural hospitals to bigger medical centers for special care. And heart patients also need help fast. A damaged heart is very dangerous, and speed is always important.

For all those patients whose lives are in danger, the helicopter team is a lifesaving team.

Buckling up before takeoff takes on new meaning for a patient on board a med-evac chopper.

WHEN EVERY SECOND COUNTS

MOTORCYCLES

Sometimes smaller is better when it comes to getting help to someone in need. In some big cities, where the streets are often choked with heavy traffic, EMTs turn to motorcycles. After all, an ambulance stuck in gridlock cannot help someone who is hurt or ill. Speedy treatment saves lives, and these rescue cycles can cut response time in half. Packed in the carrying cases in the back are airway openers, oxygen, and other lifesavers.

AIRPLANES

In areas where the nearest hospital can be a great distance away, airplanes double as ambulances. Many doctors in these areas have pilot's licenses and will gladly fly a patient to more intensive help.

FLYING DOCTORS OF AMERICA

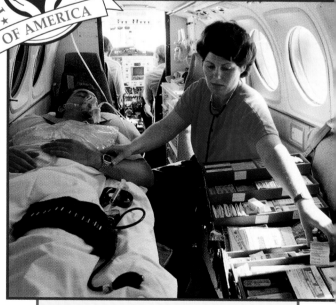

Small spaces, big challenges. A flying doctor keeps a close watch on a seriously ill patient, medicines at the ready.

Into the ER

Sirens wail. Lights flash. An ambulance races toward the hospital. Within seconds, a stretcher is unloaded and wheeled swiftly through the doors marked EMERGENCY. The EMTs speak quickly to the waiting medical team— terse words describing the victim's condition. What will happen next?

There will be over 90 million visits to America's emergency rooms this year. People will go with fishhooks stuck in thumbs, with wrists broken playing basketball. They will hobble in with sprained ankles and complain of stomachaches after summer picnics. Waiting to help them, 24 hours a day, 365 days a year, is a team of fiercely dedicated men and women.

What happens behind the ER doors? What does it take to save a life?

GIVE ME THE BULLET!

When EMTs wheel a patient into the ER, they have only a few seconds to let the ER team know about a patient's vital signs (see pp. 24–25) and condition. It's called GIVING THE BULLET, because it has to be fast and well-aimed. Time is always precious in the ER, as doctors and nurses juggle up to 15 cases at a time. Each ER team might see 40 or 50 patients in a single day. Busy hospitals see about 45,000 patients a year.

BROKEN LEG IN EIGHT. CHEST PAIN IN FOUR. DIZZY WITH FEVER IN SIX.

The very worst cases go right in, but most patients see the TRIAGE NURSE first. Triage means "sort," and it is that person's job to sort out who needs the most help. To do this he or she puts each patient into one of three categories.
EMERGENT—Patients who have been in major accidents with multiple injuries, people with chest pains or severe allergic reactions. Their conditions could worsen at any moment.
URGENT—Patients with high fevers or badly broken limbs.
ROUTINE—Patients with complaints such as earaches or sore throats that are better treated in a doctor's office. They might have to wait a long time.

QUESTIONS AND ANSWERS

Being a doctor is a bit like being a detective. There is a mystery to solve and clues that lead to the answer. Information has to be gathered; a lot of questions get asked; and a suspect has to be identified—the answer to what's wrong. Sometimes it can get very tricky. One illness can masquerade as another. For example, sometimes a painful shoulder can be a sign of a heart attack.

CODE BLUE! GET THE TRAUMA TEAM!

The most critically ill patients need the help of more than one person. When someone with multiple injuries is brought in, a whole group gets to work. They are called the TRAUMA TEAM and each has a job to do. The AIRWAY TEAM will worry only about the patient's breathing. The ASSESSMENT TEAM will try to figure out what's wrong. The SUPPORT TEAM helps make things happen. The pace is intense. Every second is precious as the teams struggle to stay one step ahead of disaster. How do they do it? Read on.

TALK LIKE AN ER DOC

The ER team has a whole slew of secret words that it uses on the job. Here are some of the most common.

PLAYER—A patient.

TRAIN WRECK—A "player" with multiple injuries or diseases.

CODE—When a "train wreck's" heart has stopped. Also called a CODE BLUE or CODE RED.

SCUT MONKEY—A medical student assigned to all the most unpleasant jobs in the ER, called SCUT WORK.

MEET 'EM, GREET 'EM, TREAT 'EM, AND STREET 'EM—The fast treatment and speedy release of patients.

BURNING DAYLIGHT—Taking too long to complete a procedure.

BUG JUICE—Intravenous antibiotics.

Even a routine broken ankle is never really routine. Every patient is different, every case unique.

Band-Aids are great for minor cuts. Tylenol is fine for a headache. But when things really go wrong, you need a lot more than first-aid cream!

12 Things Every ER Needs

1. Diagnostic Tools

Basic devices for listening to and looking at a patient's body. STETHOSCOPES are used to hear heart and lungs, intestines and blood vessels. (See p. 25.) BLOOD-PRESSURE CUFFS measure the heart's ability to move blood through the body. PENLIGHTS shine into stuffed-up ears and sore throats, and check the pupils of the eyes. (See p. 25.) TONGUE DEPRESSORS help keep tongues out of the way for a peek at tender tonsils. OPTHALMOSCOPES provide a peek at eye-insides.

2. An EKG Machine and Heart Monitor

The heart has an electrical current that keeps it beating properly. By attaching sensors to different parts of the patient's body, the ER team can get a picture of how the heart is working. That picture is called an ELECTROCARDIOGRAM (ee-**lek**-trow-**kar**-dee-o-gram). Heart monitors keep a constant eye on the body's functions and display the results on a small TV screen.

3. Protective Clothing

Blood can carry disease. The ER staff needs protection from germs that might be spread by a patient. The patients also need protection from any germs the ER staff might have. Eyeglasses, masks, gloves, and gowns do the trick. (See pp. 20-21.)

4. An X-Ray Machine

Patients too injured to be moved can still have their bones examined to see if they are broken. These "see-through" machines can wheel right to the patients' bedsides.

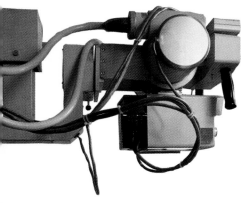

5. Gurneys

Strong yet easy-to-move beds transport patients from the ER to the other parts of the hospital.

6. Wheelchairs

Patients with less serious injuries get around in these during their stay in the ER.

8. Suture Kits

Stitching up cuts is a common task in the ER. These sterile kits come complete with everything docs need to make sewing a snap. There are over 100 different weights of thread available, for suturing tiny blood vessels to sewing up a head wound. Staples and a special glue are also used, depending on the wound.

7. Blood-Drawing Equipment

Sometimes the secret to what makes us sick is locked in our blood. The type of blood has to be identified when a patient is bleeding heavily and needs new blood. Blood samples are drawn from a vein and sent to the lab for a microscopic investigation. (See pp. 26-27.)

9. Casting Equipment

Broken bones need to be kept from moving. Using a soft cotton wrapping, topped with a quick-drying, plaster-soaked gauze, doctors will brace and protect the broken limb.

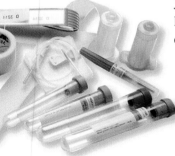

10. Crash Carts

When a patient starts to "crash"— the heart stopping or lungs not working—the ER staff turns to this rolling cart that is packed with lifesaving equipment—breathing tubes to open up blocked airways, DEFIBRILLATORS to jolt hearts that are beating poorly—or not at all—back into action, SUCTION DEVICES that work like little vacuum cleaners, perfect for when blood or mucus blocks airways or interferes with a doctor's ability to treat a patient, SCALPELS for cutting the skin, and more.

11. A Highly Trained Medical Team

The best equipment is useless without a dedicated team to use it. There *is* no ER without the doctors, nurses, physician's assistants, technicians, social workers, clinical assistants, and administrators who staff it.

12. Most important? The three Cs: Care, Compassion, & Commitment.

Gloved and

Are EMTs, doctors, and nurses afraid of their patients? Sometimes it might seem that way. They hide behind masks. They wear plastic eye shields. They always wear gloves. Every inch of their bodies is covered with at least two layers before touching a patient in the operating room. Why?

SCRUB CAP _____

FACE MASK _____

SURGICAL GOWN _____

PROTECTIVE LATEX _____
GLOVES

Street clothes are never worn into the OR. The medical staff strips down to their underwear, then pulls on clothing that has been washed in extremely hot water with germ-killing soaps. The first layer pulled on is the SCRUB SUIT, shown below. Surgeons and certain nurses will add a SURGICAL GOWN and GLOVES, seen at the right.

SCRUB CAP _____→

SCRUB
SHIRT _____→

PLASTIC FACE
SHIELD

It's important to keep splattered blood out of the doctor's eyes. A plastic face shield deflects fluids and adds an extra layer of protection to the cloth face mask and protective glasses.

SCRUB PANTS _____→

Special magnifying glasses offer a larger-than-life view of the body's nooks and crannies.

Gowned

CLEAN-AIR HOOD

During certain types of surgery, an extra level of protection is needed for the patient's safety. Surgeons don helmets that contain a suction tube that pulls exhaust away from the body. Clean air enters from the bottom of the suit. In typical operating room garb, everything from the shoulders up is non-sterile. But with a clean-air suit, the face mask and head are sterile. That way, no germs can escape into the air, and then, into the patient's body.

BIOHAZARD SUIT

The ultimate in protection. Multiple puncture-proof layers with a self-contained air supply protect medical workers against deadly air-borne viruses like EBOLA.

SHOE COVERS

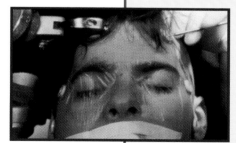

A sleeping patient's eyes are sometimes covered with plastic wrap for protection during anesthesia. (See p. 23.)

SCRUB-A-DUB-DUB

The strictest barriers to bacteria are thrown up in the operating room. Because deep incisions into the patient's skin are made, germs can rush in. Doctors and nurses take extra care to protect patients from being exposed to those germs. When the surgical team gets ready for surgery, hands are washed for five to ten minutes. Each finger has four sides, and each side will be scrubbed with a bacteria-killing soap and a stiff brush. Hands are held up after rinsing so the germy water drains away from the fingertips.

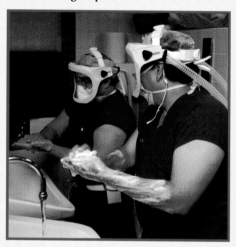

PROTECTING THE PATIENT

The same care that goes into dressing the surgical team applies to the patient, too. Every item that comes in contact with the patient must be free of germs. Sterile sheets are draped over the patient, leaving only the area being operated on exposed.

That patch of skin is painted with an antibacterial liquid called BETADINE, to kill any germs that might travel from the skin into the body during an operation.

Patients having GENERAL ANESTHESIA, which puts them into a deep sleep, even have their closed eyes covered with gauze pads or plastic wrap and taped shut. This is because under anesthesia the body stops producing the fluids that moisten the eyes. Even the tiniest exposure to air will dry the delicate tissue. The tape forms an airtight seal.

Welcome to the Pit

Sometimes it's as simple as a crying baby with an earache. Sometimes it's a young person who's just been in a bad car accident. Sometimes it's a frail grandmother who feels like a hippo is sitting on her chest.

Sometimes the patient is nice. Sometimes the patient is nasty. And yet, for the people who work in the emergency room, every patient is the same. They all need help.

Is there something wrong with the patient's lungs? This ER doctor scans a chest X ray looking for trouble.

The people who work in the ER sometimes call it "the pit," and you have to be really tough to work there. What's a typical day like in the pit? For one thing, every day is completely different from the day before. Imagine for a moment that you work there. Here's a taste of life behind the door marked EMERGENCY.

NO TIME TO EAT. NO TIME TO REST.

Everything happens super-fast in the ER. When the weather is bad, or at times when most doctors' offices are closed, things get even busier. Weekends and holidays are always wild.

Your shift begins at six in the morning, and as you grab a quick cup of coffee, the doctors and nurses going home brief you quickly about the patients still being treated.

Those doctors and nurses have had a rough night. They had to deal with a multi-vehicle car accident with lots of injuries, and they're exhausted. The ER team always has to do their best even if they are so tired they can hardly stand. They try to remember patients' names, but when things get rushed and they get tired, they sometimes give up and refer to them by their ailments—the "chest pain in bed eight" or the "broken wrist in bed two."

Once you know what's going on with the patients already being treated, you review the triage nurse's notes on the new patients—a little girl with stomach pains, a grandfather with a bad cough, and a 14-year-old who slipped and now has an ankle swollen to the size of an elephant's. It's time to start helping your patients.

WHAT'S ON THE BOARD?

A giant blackboard keeps track of which patient is in what room, along with the doctor and nurse responsible for the patients' care. New names are added and old ones erased as patients are sent home or moved upstairs for a longer stay in the hospital.

WHERE TO BEGIN?

The care of a patient always begins with a series of questions. Where does it hurt? When did it start? Has this ever happened before? You begin with the child complaining of stomach pains. Your questions are the start of a PATIENT HISTORY and it's all written down on her CHART, a sheaf of papers on a clipboard that will track every detail of her care. Her symptoms—a tenderness in the belly, a low fever, and a high white blood count, confirmed by a blood test—are classic markers of appendicitis, and with that diagnosis made, you call a surgeon, and the little girl is whisked off to surgery.

Many times, patients who are brought into the ER can't answer those questions or tell the ER team what hurts because they are UNCONSCIOUS—their brains are not getting enough blood to run their bodies properly or they have been given strong medications that dull the alertness centers of the brain. But even when patients can't talk, their bodies can. You will order up LABS for most patients, which are a series of tests that show what's happening inside. (See pp. 26-27.)

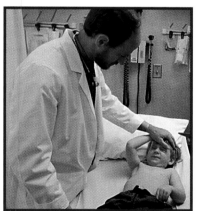

INSIDE THE ER

You spend a lot of time at the CENTRAL DESK. That's the brain and heart of the ER. It is set up so that the most seriously ill patients are close by, where you can keep a watchful eye on them. The staff makes phone calls and chart entries and holds quick conferences here.

The grandfather with the bad cough is hooked up to a machine that measures his heartbeat, pulse, and blood pressure, as well as the amount of oxygen in his blood. A chest X ray and several blood tests confirm the diagnosis of what you believe is probably pneumonia, a serious lung infection. You decide to ADMIT him to the upper floors of the hospital for treatment. You send the young man with the swollen ankle to have an X ray but his films show no breaks. He has a bad sprain. It is wrapped and iced, and he is DISCHARGED, sent home to recover.

12 HOURS. 45 PATIENTS.

Patients come and go. The hours melt away. Lunchtime comes, but it's too hectic for more than a bite of stale doughnut at the desk. All day, you ease pains and fix what's broken. You put in stitches, set snapped bones, wrap sprains, and prescribe medicines to fight infections. You listen to what the patients tell you, but you also "hear" with your eyes, looking for more clues to what might be wrong. And along the way you manage to smile and joke and put your patients at ease.

HELP FROM THE KITCHEN

Medicine today depends on lots of complicated and expensive machinery. But surprisingly, some common everyday household objects can also be real lifesavers.

PLASTIC WRAP— Yes, it keeps food fresh in the fridge, but it also comes in very handy out in the field and in the OR. EMTs use it to cover really bad wounds. And during surgery, when eyes need to be covered because of the effects of the drugs that put people to sleep, plastic wrap works perfectly. (See p. 21.)

KRAZY GLUE—It can hold a piano to the ceiling, but it's also great for reattaching tiny little blood vessels, too delicate to be sewn shut. Surgeons sometimes use Krazy Glue in microsurgery on the hand.

TURKEY BASTERS—Emergency medical workers swear by these devices. When fluids collect in the mouth and throat, these quickly suck them away.

Vital Signs

A LARYNGOSCOPE (lar-**in**-joe-scope) holds the tongue down and lights the way so emergency medical workers can insert an ET tube.

A heartbeat. A pulse. Blood rushing through our veins. These are the simple markers of human life. Out in the field, as the lights flash and the radios crackle, they are the first things the paramedics listen for. And in the ER, where the pace is fast and the action furious, where machines beep and gurneys hurtle up and down the hallways, the care of a patient begins with the gentlest of actions…a touch of a fingertip on a wrist.

They are called the signs of life. Any examination of a patient starts with a search for these signs that the heart, lungs, and other organs of the body are working as they should. Here's how they do it.

LOOK AND LISTEN

Seeing, hearing, feeling, touching, and smelling…our senses are sometimes the best tool for finding out what's wrong. The very first thing EMTs or ER team members do is take a close look at the patient, checking for signs of injury or unusual breathing. They feel for tenderness, spasms, heat, or cold; listen for changes in breathing or the grating sounds of broken bones; stay alert to odd smells coming from the breath, body, or clothing of the patient. They look for anything that doesn't seem right. Sometimes the problem is obvious. Sometimes they can't see anything wrong.

PULSE IS 65 AND IRREGULAR

Checking a patient's pulse will tell how well a person's heart is beating. A healthy adult heart beats about 60 to 80 times a minute when the person is sitting still. Children's hearts beat faster. Very strong athletes usually have a slower heartbeat. The rule of thumb is anything over 100 or under 60 beats per minute means trouble (for school-age kids the range is between 70 and 110 beats while resting). Besides the number of times the heart beats, medics will also be listening for the rhythm and force of those beats. Are they even and well spaced or are they irregular? Is the pulse weak and hard to feel or is it pounding far too fast?

A PULSE OXIMETER is a small device that clips onto a fingertip. It sends a beam of light through the skin to tell if there is enough oxygen circulating in the blood. It is always used for patients who are having trouble breathing. A reading of less than 95% can be a sign of trouble.

BP IS 150 OVER 90!

BLOOD PRESSURE, called BP for short, is a sign of how well the heart is moving blood through the body. Medics will listen for two important moments in the heartbeat cycle. The higher number tells how hard the blood is pushing against the walls of the blood vessels when the heart contracts, the lower one, when the heart relaxes between beats. When someone's BP is too low, it means that blood may not be getting to the brain. A high reading means the heart is working too hard.

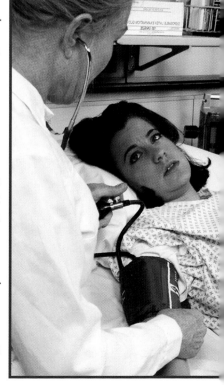

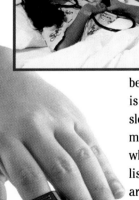

RESPIRATIONS ARE 16

How is the patient breathing? Is she taking even breaths? Struggling to draw in air? Making odd sounds with each inhalation? If a person is not breathing well, that means oxygen will not be able to get to the brain. The average person takes between 10 and 20 breaths per minute. Children breathe faster. Too fast or too slow means trouble. Extra oxygen can help, and when the passageway between the mouth and lungs is blocked, an ENDOTRACHEAL (en-doe-**tray**-key-ul) TUBE (called an ET TUBE for short) can be inserted through the mouth and down into the throat to help air get to the lungs.

WEIGHT? 110. TEMPERATURE? 99.2

To give the proper dosages of medicines, paramedics and doctors must know the size of the patient. A big person needs more medicine than a small one. The patient's temperature will also be checked. Anything above 99 probably means the body is fighting an infection, although it can also be a sign of overheating.

PUPILS ARE UNEQUAL AND DILATED

Eyes can tell a lot about health. The pupil, the black hole in the center of the eye, DILATES (gets bigger) or CONSTRICTS (gets smaller) depending on how much light is coming in. The pupils should be the same size and they should get smaller when a light is shined at them. When pupils don't act normally, it can be a sign that the brain or eye has been injured.

THE SKIN IS COOL AND CLAMMY

What color is the patient's skin? How does it feel? If it feels cold and damp, that's a clear sign of shock. (See p. 11.) A blue tinge shows lack of oxygen. A yellow cast indicates liver problems. When a person has dark skin, medics look for color changes around the lips, under fingernails, on the palms and earlobes, and in the whites of the eyes.

What Are <u>Your</u> Vital Signs ?

Basic vital signs include PULSE, RESPIRATION, BLOOD PRESSURE, and TEMPERATURE. You can't check your blood pressure without a special medical instrument, but you can monitor the others.

Start with your PULSE. Press your fingertip on your wrist just below the thumb until you feel a gentle throb. Look at a clock with a second hand and count the number of beats for thirty seconds. Multiply by two and you have your pulse rate. (For example, 40 beats in 30 seconds means you have a pulse of 80.)

Now, check your RESPS. Looking at a clock with a second hand, count the number of times you inhale (take a breath) in 30 seconds. Breathe normally. Then multiply that number by two. (For example, 8 breaths in 30 seconds means your resps are 16.)

VITAL TOOLS

For most medical workers, the most-turned-to tool is the STETHOSCOPE, an amplifier for all the strange sounds our bodies make.

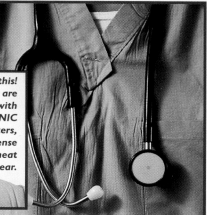

Now hear this! Temperatures are taken with TYMPANIC thermometers, which sense the heat in your ear.

Hearts aren't the only things the ER team listens to. Lungs are checked, along with blood vessels and, surprisingly, the stomach and intestines. Using a stethoscope, doctors can hear irregular heartbeats, irritated airways, and blockages in the digestive tract. It's also used with a blood-pressure cuff to monitor blood pressure. This little tool can definitely save lives. By the way, the medical term for listening to body sounds is AUSCULTATION (as-kul-**tay**-shun).

Before 1816, when a man named RENE LAENNEC invented the stethoscope, doctors used to lay an ear against the part they wanted to listen to.

Another must-have for medical workers is a blood-pressure kit. Its proper medical name is a SPHYGMOMANOMETER (**sfig**-mow-man-**om**-e-ter). The cuff part comes in kid and grown-up sizes. For very tiny babies, there are cuffs the size of a Band-Aid.

A third handy tool is an OTOSCOPE, perfect for peering into eyes, ears, and throats. It has a built-in light for easy viewing.

A stomachache that has lasted for days. A sharp pain in the knee that just won't go away. A painful twinge every time a breath is taken. Clearly there is something wrong. But how can doctors diagnose the problem without being able to see inside?

Get Me a Chem 7!

Round up the usual suspects! That's what busy ER doctors say when treating a patient who has just come in. Who or what are those suspects? Let's find out.

BLOOD BASICS

A technician called a PHLEBOTOMIST (fle-**bott**-uh-mist) draws blood from a patient's vein and fills several test tubes with it. It might look like a lot of blood, but it's really only two tablespoons full. Each test tube has a different color lid on it, and some tubes contain different chemicals. The blue-topped tube, for example, has a drug that prepares the blood so its clotting ability can be measured.

The blood is brought to the laboratory, where highly trained LAB TECHNICIANS, using complex computerized machines, figure out what's going on. Blood is like a river that flows through our bodies. The watery fluid is called PLASMA, and floating in it are sugars and minerals that nourish every organ and muscle.

That fast-flowing river also carries the blood's three main ingredients. RED CELLS carry oxygen through our bodies. WHITE CELLS fight infection. PLATELETS, filled with fibrin, help to "tie up" damaged blood cells and form clots when we bleed. The lab techs test every part of the blood. The picture above shows what it all looks like when a technician peers into a microscope.

"Get me a rainbow." That's how doctors ask for a full set of blood chemistries.

I NEED A CBC

The first test up is the COMPLETE BLOOD COUNT. The technician loads a blood sample into a machine that counts the number of red cells, white cells, and platelets. The red blood cells are the first counted. Too few mean the patient needs a TRANSFUSION, extra blood pumped into his or her body. Another test called a CRIT (short for hematocrit) will measure what percentage of the blood is made of red cells. At least 40% of the blood should be red cells.

Baby's first picture. This ultrasound image of an unborn child allows doctors to see if all's well.

...AND A CROSS MATCH

An accident victim is bleeding badly and needs a transfusion. But blood comes in different types, A, B, AB, and O. It also has two Rh types—positive and negative. If the wrong type of blood is given, the body will react badly. If there is time, doctors will always try to get the right type. But luckily, almost everyone can tolerate O negative blood. It's known as the UNIVERSAL DONOR. The problem is, only 7% of the population has this blood type, so supplies are hard to come by.

Spin, then search. A centrifuge isolates different parts of the blood for study under a microscope.

DON'T FORGET A WBC, PT/PTT, AND COAG

Besides counting red cells, the technician also counts white blood cells (WBC). Too many white cells are a sign of infection. Platelets need to be counted, too. A PT/PTT (short for prothrombin time/partial thromboplastin time) will tell how quickly the blood will be able to clot. A COAG checks for the chemicals needed to make the blood coagulate, or clot.

I'LL NEED A CHEM 7 AND LYTES, TOO!

What about plasma, the watery fluid that holds all the blood cells? Is there anything in it that can help tell about a patient's condition? Technicians look for four basic chemicals—sodium, potassium, chloride, and bicarbonate. Those are LYTES, short for electrolytes. There are three other chemical compounds suspended in plasma—glucose (a kind of sugar), BUN (short for blood urea nitrogen), and something called creatinine (cree-**at**-in-ine). Too little or too much of any of these can lead to heart problems. An abundance can indicate kidney damage.

LET'S CHECK THE OTHER FLUIDS

Even those body leftovers that usually end up getting flushed down the toilet tell a lot about someone's medical condition. And as unpleasant as it sounds, studying bathroom by-products can show if the patient is bleeding internally.

What does that mean? If a patient has a cut arm, the ER team can easily see it. But if the internal organs are hurt (which can happen with a really bad fall), no one can see the damage. Blood in the urine or stool tells them that a person is bleeding on the inside. The ER team will order up a UA, short for urinalysis, and when needed, a GUAIAC—a stool sample that can show the presence of blood. Doctors think of pee as liquid gold because it can tell so much about a patient's general health—over a dozen vital clues that can reveal major illnessess.

Taking Pictures with Sound

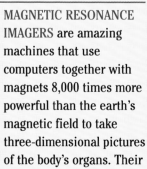

Sound can produce a picture, too. ULTRASOUND uses high-frequency sound waves (way above what we can hear) aimed at a part of the body. The sound strikes the body and bounces back to form a picture. It's perfect for peeking at babies still in the womb, as well as searching for signs of infection in livers, bladders, and other body parts. It can also reveal small stones in gall bladders and kidneys. Best of all, it doesn't hurt a bit!

LET'S GET A PICTURE!

ER teams frequently order up pictures of injured or tender areas. These are the most often asked for.

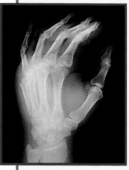

X RAYS

When a small amount of radiation passes through the body and hits a sensitive film on the other side, an image is left on the film. Bones show up as white shapes because the X rays can't get through the calcium that makes up the bones. Soft-tissue organs, like lungs, show up as black shapes against gray. Pictures of the lungs, a chest X ray called a CXR in ER-talk, are the most often asked for.

CT SCANS

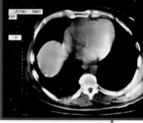

When X rays meet up with computers, the end result is COMPUTED TOMOGRAPHY. CT images show the organs of the body, one slice at a time. The patient lies on a table surrounded by a large doughnut ring. X-ray beams rotate around the patient, producing slice-by-slice pictures of the affected part. The computer generates an image by combining the slices.

MRIs

MAGNETIC RESONANCE IMAGERS are amazing machines that use computers together with magnets 8,000 times more powerful than the earth's magnetic field to take three-dimensional pictures of the body's organs. Their pictures offer extremely detailed views of soft tissue that CT machines might miss.

An operating room is a thrilling place to be— a real-life version of a life-or-death video game, a place where one wrong move can end up with a big flashing light that says GAME OVER. But this is no game. Somebody's life is on the line. Surgery is *always* exciting.

Under the Knife

PROBES
Used to move delicate tissue aside so problem areas can be studied.

SUTURING INSTRUMENTS
NEEDLE HOLDERS hold the needle. LIGATURE CARRIERS help to thread the sutures around blood vessels and organs.

CLAMPS
Two kinds. One type controls blood flow. The other holds skin and tissue out of the way.

RETRACTORS
Look a bit like little rakes and are used to pull back a part of the body, such as the flesh at the edge of an incision.

FORCEPS
TWEEZERS FORCEPS hold delicate tissue or the sutures that close wounds. THUMB FORCEPS are used to hold the most delicate tissue. TOOTHED TISSUE FORCEPS hold thicker tissue. SCISSORS FORCEPS are used to hold skin out of the way during surgery, and SPONGE FORCEPS are used for… you guessed it, holding on to sponges!

SCALPELS
Ultra-sharp blades on an easy-to-handle handle. These are used to make a cut in the skin, called an incision, so doctors can get to the heart of the problem.

SCISSORS
Two kinds with incredibly sharp blades. These SUTURE SCISSORS cut the thread doctors stitch wounds shut with. DISSECTION SCISSORS come in all sizes from teeny (for use in delicate eye surgery) to big for cutting through tough muscle.

Sliding into home plate, the ball player got more than she bargained for. Along with a home run, she ended up with a COMPOUND FRACTURE of the bone below her knee. In this type of break, the bone snaps and pierces the skin. She will need the help of a SURGEON, a specially trained doctor who will fix her broken leg.

THE DEEPEST CUT

Sometimes, a patient needs to be moved from the ER to the OR (short for OPERATING ROOM). There, surgeons cut open the skin to reach deep into the body. They might REMOVE parts that are infected, perhaps an inflamed appendix or tonsils. They might REPAIR a part that has been damaged, such as a heart valve. They might even REPLACE a part that no longer functions, such as a kidney.

Skin keeps germs out of our bodies. When the skin is cut, the protective barrier is broken. Microbes can creep in and cause infections. It is extremely important to keep everything as clean as possible. Surgeons must scrub every inch of every finger on each hand for over five minutes and pull on several layers of protective clothing. (See p. 21.)

IN THE OR

There are two teams in the OR waiting to fix the young woman's broken bone. Only those who have been through that five-minute scrub and have donned an extra layer of protective clothing will actually touch the patient. They are the CHIEF SURGEON, a team of assistants, and a SCRUB NURSE, whose job it is to make sure that everything they touch is clean, clean, clean. Together they are called the SCRUBBED STERILE TEAM.

But they can't do everything by themselves. They are joined by a second group called the UNSCRUBBED UNSTERILE TEAM. That doesn't mean they've been playing in the mud. They wear much of the same protective clothing but they don't scrub up as vigorously.

THIS WON'T HURT A BIT

The unscrubbed unsterile team has a special doctor at the helm, called an ANESTHESIOLOGIST (an-ess-**thee**-zee-ol-o-jist). He or she will make sure that the patient cannot feel any pain during surgery. To do this, these doctors use very powerful drugs, called ANESTHETICS, which put the patient into a deep sleep or make the area being operated on numb. The patient must then be closely watched at every second to make sure heartbeat and breathing are okay.

Another vital member of this team is the CIRCULATING NURSE. This person is responsible for bringing extra supplies from outside the sterile area and for staying with the patient during the recovery from surgery.

SCALPEL. RETRACTOR. GARBAGE.

Using special tools, the surgeons get to work the minute the patient is asleep. Because the young woman's bone has broken in several places, they decide to pin it using a stainless-steel bar with screw holes in it. This will brace the bone and hold it in place as it heals.

Surgeons depend on their tools (see the tray at left). Here are some other must-haves.

MAYO STAND—A little table that holds all the instruments, placed next to the patient.

KICK BUCKETS—There is a surprising amount of garbage produced during surgery. These hold used sponges, which have absorbed the blood. Nothing else can be thrown in.

OXYGEN AND OTHER GASES—Breathing aids and anesthetics are stored in holding tanks built directly into the walls.

SURGERY SAMPLER

Sometimes an injury or illness needs a new kind of surgery. These are some of the most common.

ARTHROSCOPIC SURGERY

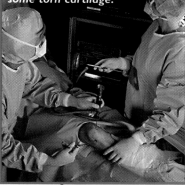
What's on TV? A surgeon checks the screen before snipping some torn cartilage.

Joints like knees and shoulders are best fixed with ARTHROSCOPY. Doctors put a teeny camera with a cutting tool attached into a very small cut near the injured area. The surgeon then watches a TV screen to see what's happening inside.

LASER SURGERY

Fragile, tiny areas, like eyes, are best fixed using a special tool that sends out a pinpoint of laser light to penetrate delicate tissue and seal blood vessels so there is no bleeding.

PLASTIC SURGERY

This type of surgery has nothing to do with plastic. Plastic surgeons rebuild or reshape parts of the body, especially on the face. They also do skin grafts, replacing sections of skin that have been damaged by burns.

Brrr. It's Freezing!

The OR is usually kept quite cool. But in many cases the patients are wearing nothing more than a sheet. What gives? It's done to keep the surgeons comfortable in their layers of scrubs. Unfortunately it's not the best for the patients, and the new recommendation is to turn up the heat.

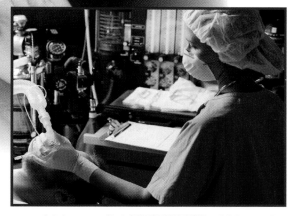

A respirator "breathes" for a critically ill patient as a doctor carefully listens to the breath sounds.

Tales from the ICU

CONSTANT CARE

The drama that began with a call for help continues. After the ambulance has sped to the scene…after the victim has been rushed to the ER…after lifesaving surgery…the patient still needs a lot of care. Constant care. The kind of care that can be found in only one place.

A young man fell off his roof while fixing a loose shingle. Broken ribs injured his lungs and he bled a lot internally. He spent over four hours in the operating room and has been in the recovery room for over two hours. But he is still having a hard time breathing, and a decision is made to put him on a VENTILATOR, a machine that will help him to breathe. He needs to be watched constantly, his heart rate and pulse monitored carefully, his temperature checked frequently. He needs someone to be close at hand at all times, just in case he should take a turn for the worse. He needs the men and women of the INTENSIVE CARE UNIT.

Mission Control. Looking a bit like a NASA scientist, a nurse keeps a watchful eye on a dozen patients at a time, while computers monitor every heartbeat.

CRITICAL CONDITION

Most hospitals have a special area where they care for their sickest patients. Here, doctors and nurses keep a constant eye on those people whose condition might change at any moment. People who have just had heart attacks, people who are breathing with the help of respirators, and even people who seem okay but who have life-threatening conditions such as head injuries will be moved here. Each intensive care unit (called ICU for short) is built around a central control station. Every bed is linked to a series of computer screens where a member of the nursing staff can tell at a glance how each patient is doing. The heartbeat and pulse of each and every patient is always on display on the screen.

In some hospitals, people with heart problems are placed in a special ICU called the CORONARY CARE UNIT (CCU). The team there is headed up by a CARDIOLOGIST, a doctor who specializes in dealing with ailing hearts.

SPECIAL CARE FOR THE LITTLEST ONES

Sometimes, babies are born too soon, before they are big enough to survive outside the protection of their mothers' bodies. Sometimes these premature babies are born with heart problems or other illnesses. Special ICUs, called NICUs (the N is for *neonate,* which means "just-born") help teeny babies receive the care they need to grow bigger and get better.

Completely enclosed cribs called INCUBATORS keep babies warm and protect them from germs. Tiny ventilators help get oxygen into their bodies until their little lungs can work by themselves.

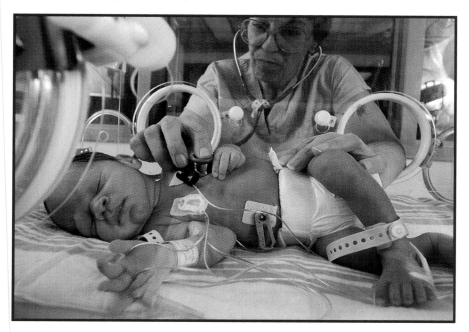

TRUE LIFESAVERS

DEFIB!

Out in the field during a rescue, in the ER as treatment begins, and especially in the ICU, doctors depend on a small box with a big charge.

In a healthy person, each heartbeat begins with an electrical impulse. During CARDIAC ARREST the powerful muscles of the heart completely stop contracting. In FIBRILLATION (fib-rill-**ay**-shun) the heart beats irregularly. But even a stopped heart can be shocked back into a normal rhythm by a powerful jolt of electricity.

DEFIBRILLATORS work by resetting the rhythm of the heart to the proper beat by sending an electric shock through the chest wall. It's a bit like a jump start for a car. Two metal plates that have been rubbed in a special gel, which ER teams call "goop," are placed on the patient's chest. A yell of "Clear!" goes out just before the electricity surges through the paddles, and everyone except the person holding the paddles steps away from the patient. Anyone touching the patient when that jolt of electricity is delivered would be knocked clear across the room and probably knocked out cold as well. Sometimes it takes over 20 shocks to restore a patient's heart rhythm.

Doctors Without

There are places where the nearest hospital is a hundred miles away… jungles with only rivers for roadways…vast deserts hours from civilization. Who cares for the people who live here? What happens when they need help?

Hours from the nearest hospital, a flying doctor in Kenya, Africa, is greeted by her needy patients.

From Alaska to Africa doctors climb into airplanes to reach the needy. In areas torn by war, medics work in quickly raised tents in fields of mud. As natural disasters such as floods and earthquakes rip apart the earth, doctors and nurses rush to help the injured. Wherever people live, no matter how remote, medical help is always needed. Here are some glimpses of medical miracle-workers.

DOCTORS WITH WINGS

Two weeks every month, a doctor in Kenya brings new meaning to the word "house calls" by taking to the sky in her Piper Cherokee aircraft. She has logged over a million miles and has a patient load of 30,000 tribespeople. She treats everything from malaria (a disease carried by mosquitoes) to spear wounds. And she is not alone. In remote regions of the Arctic, the Australian Outback, and other isolated areas, flying doctors are the only doctors.

HOSPITALS IN THE SKY

From the outside it looks like an ordinary airplane. But inside the jet that belongs to PROJECT ORBIS—an organization devoted to restoring sight to those who have gone blind—you'll find a complete operating room, a laser treatment area, a recovery room, a teaching classroom and a well-stocked library. That's because this is the world's only flying teaching hospital. Its crew spends about 90% of the year flying to developing nations, teaching surgical techniques to native doctors.

Aboard the Project Orbis jet, surgeons perform delicate eye surgery.

Borders

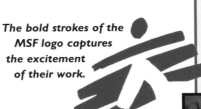

The bold strokes of the MSF logo captures the excitement of their work.

Hope arrives on horseback as an MSF doctor brings much-needed medicine to a remote corner of Afghanistan.

JUNGLE BEAT

There is a lot more to medical care then high-tech machines and state-of-the-art equipment. For some diseases, the most powerful weapons can be small doses of antibiotics or a simple mixture of sugar and salt, to restore the fluid balance after a severe bout of vomiting. Organizations such as the RED CROSS and the WORLD HEALTH ORGANIZATION send trained medical people all across the globe to help. By boat and by bicycle, by helicopter and by plane, these dedicated health-care workers bring vaccines, drugs, and hope to far-flung corners of the globe.

THE FLOATING HOSPITAL

PROJECT HOPE began with $150 and a dream. In 1958, Dr. William Walsh took an old Navy hospital ship and refitted it as a floating medical center. He headed out to the South Pacific, a place with few doctors. When the boat pulled in to its first stop, thousands were waiting on the dock to be helped.

The boat is gone, but the work continues. Each year Project Hope helps over a million people on five continents.

BORDERS

MEDICINS SANS FRONTIÈRES or MSF, which means "doctors without borders" was started in 1971 by a group of former Red Cross doctors who wanted to deliver first-rate medical care to people in distress. They wanted to serve victims of natural and man-made disasters and, especially, victims of war. It has grown to become the world's largest independent medical relief organization and has been nominated for the Nobel Peace Prize many times.

The doctors and nurses of this organization work with people who have lost their homes because of political troubles and in countries hit hard by wars. They are often the first on the scene in places hit by hurricanes, earthquakes, and floods. And in developing countries, they work in hospitals, teaching local doctors so those countries can build strong medical systems of their own.

MSF doctors and nurses work under dangerous, difficult, and constantly changing conditions, performing surgery in makeshift tents with limited supplies. They do it all for the love of medicine and do not get paid, receiving only food and shelter in exchange for their hard work.

Even in the Amazon, the doctor tells you to say "Ah." Here, a visiting medic checks on a sore throat.

WAR ZONES

Emergency medicine was born on the battlefields. (See pp. 38-39.) And sadly, the need still continues. Portable ERs and ORs, packed into big containers that can be airlifted by helicopter, bring hope and help to those in need.

One of the first of the international relief organizations, the floating ship Hope brought help around the world.

A rainy night when no sensible person should be out…an 18-hour shift, exhaustion and hunger haunting every movement. What goes through the minds and hearts of the men and women of the emergency medical teams?

What Does It Feel Like?

Day after day, from sunrise to sunrise, the calls just keep on coming. EMTs, paramedics, doctors, nurses, and other health-care workers have almost impossible jobs to do. Here's what they have to say about their lives in medicine.

Q. WHO ARE THE TOUGHEST PATIENTS TO WORK WITH?

A. Since so many emergency medical workers are parents themselves, sick kids always touch them in a special way. Most ambulances keep a supply of stuffed animals on board to help EMTs comfort young children who might be frightened. In the ER, the nurses always spend extra time cuddling and reassuring their youngest patients. And many doctors let kids bring a favorite stuffed animal or blanket into the OR if they need surgery. No one likes it when a child is hurt or ill.

Q. HOW DO YOU TAKE CARE OF SOMEONE WHO'S MEAN OR BAD?

A. That's one of the hardest things the ER team has to deal with. Should they give the best possible care to a known criminal? How do they keep from walking away when a patient starts yelling at them? They try to look past the personality and focus instead on simply healing a human body. They also try to remember that the patient is someone's son or daughter, or someone's father or mother. And that some people get nasty when they're scared. Remembering these things always helps.

Q. WHAT'S THE HARDEST PART OF EMERGENCY WORK?

A. Because the ER and the ambulances have to be staffed 24 hours a day, 365 days a year, many medical workers find themselves at work in the middle of the night and during holidays. To be fair, everyone takes turns working the night shifts. Still, being tired comes with the job. Spending 12 hours on your feet with barely enough time for a bathroom stop is really exhausting. In busy ERs, pagers beep constantly, and meals are grabbed from vending machines. Family events such as Thanksgiving dinner often have to be missed.

Q. IS IT EVER SCARY?

A. For the EMTs who must risk their lives working in treacherous weather or in dangerous conditions, work is sometimes very frightening. One EMT put it this way. "Imagine periods of intense boredom waiting for the next call, followed by moments of sheer terror answering it." And difficult rescues, where just reaching the victim can be a challenge, are tests of both physical and mental strength.

Q. HOW DO YOU DEAL WITH DEATH?

A. Most of the time, medicine is wonderfully rewarding. People who need help can be made well. Lives can be saved. But from time to time, no matter how hard everyone tries, it's impossible to help a patient. That's always hard for the emergency team. They meet once a week to talk about these cases, to learn from them and to be reassured that they did everything humanly possible.

Before this EMT can even begin to help an accident victim, she must first rappel down a canyon wall. Talk about scary!

IN THEIR OWN WORDS

Can You Hit the Dot on an "i" in a Moving Car?

What does an EMT face when trying to start an IV while barreling down the road at 50 miles an hour? Take a newspaper with you the next time you go for a drive. Try to touch a pencil point to a dot on an "i" in the smallest type you can find, as the car is moving. It's hard!

A paramedic describes the job like this. "We go from hanging out to total chaos in one minute flat. I always say that being an EMT involves three things. Panic, fear, and regret. Panic when the call comes in—*will I be able to help*? Fear when we get there—*what if I can't?* And regret when it's over, because helping someone is so cool!"

A nurse shares her feelings. "At the end of my shift, all I can think of is how much my feet hurt and how good my heart and soul feel."

A doctor sums it all up. "Sometimes it feels a little like a Wild West stampede here. There will be fifty people waiting in the hallways, and I'll be thinking, 'No way am I getting out of here tonight.' And then, somehow, they're all treated and sent home…and gosh that feels good!"

The Learning

How do medical workers learn to give a shot? Start an IV? Stitch up a wound? Operate on a damaged heart? So much is at stake with every medical procedure, even the simplest. One slip of the hand can easily lead to disaster. Medical workers need to know their stuff, but how can they learn without putting patients in danger?

What do Rescue Randy, Hurt-Head Harry and Trauma Tom have in common? They can bleed and breathe and yet they're all dummies! And without them, EMTs, doctors, physician's assistants, and nurses wouldn't be able to help real people when they need help.

A BAG OF BONES

How do you begin? No patient wants a beginner practicing on them. And there are so many parts of the body to learn about, all with long Latin names to remember, most of them hidden beneath the protective wrappings of our skin. Textbooks with lots of pictures help, but real flesh-and-blood people are a lot different from the printed page.

EMTs spend hundreds of hours studying and observing. They begin with simple things like learning how to perform CARDIOPULMONARY (**car**-dee-oh-**pul**-muh-nair-y) RESUSCITATION *(*ree-**sus**-uh-tay-shun*)* or CPR, which helps sustain breathing and heartbeat if either have stopped. They then move on to more difficult tasks, such as starting IV lines and opening up blocked airways.

And as hard as it is to learn what "normal" looks like, you also have to be able to know what damage you might expect. What exactly does a third-degree burn or an open fracture of the thigh bone really look like? Kits that simulate all sorts of injuries prepare student EMTs for the real thing.

Different-size people need different rescue breathing techniques. Dummies, from newborn to grown-up, teach how.

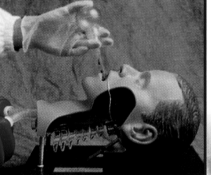

▲ *"Tubing" a patient—putting in a breathing tube—is tricky. This dummy duplicates the experience.*

◀ *Beauty is only skin deep, as this teaching skeleton shows. Underneath, an amazing network of bones, muscles, and organs keeps us ticking.*

▼ *They call him Megacode Kelly, because this dummy can have a "heart attack," "stop breathing," and "suffer" from other life-threatening problems.*

Curve

Hand-held models of hearts, detailed down to the last blood vessel, help to show each and every part.

DAWN OF THE DEAD

Medical students training to become doctors need even more intense training than EMTs. One of the ways they learn about all the nooks and crannies in a body is by carefully studying CADAVERS. These are dead bodies, usually donated by people who leave their bodies to science when they die. The bodies are treated with a special chemical called FORMALDEHYDE to keep them from decaying. It might sound gross, but it's the best way for students to learn all about anatomy. Every medical student spends up to three months carefully examining each and every part of a cadaver.

In the future, computers may replace this real-life anatomy lesson with virtual-reality tours of every part of every organ. But for now, this is the best way to learn.

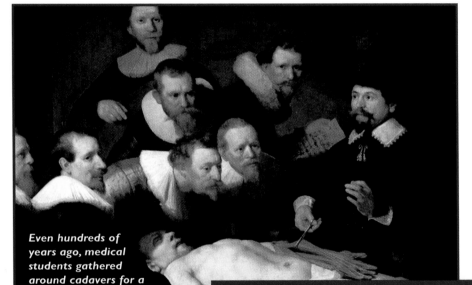

Even hundreds of years ago, medical students gathered around cadavers for a firsthand look at the amazing human body.

STARTING AT THE BOTTOM

When medical workers have learned all they can from books, models, simulations, and even dead bodies, they start learning at the hospital. First, simply watching, doing the dirtiest chores, the future EMTs, doctors, physician's assistants, and nurses begin to absorb knowledge like a sponge absorbs water. Paramedics log over 100 hours in the hospital. Some doctors spend seven years in training.

And even after many years on the job, the training doesn't stop. New developments, new tools, and better ways to save lives keep medical workers learning all the time.

Practice Makes Perfect

They do it a thousand times. With their eyes shut. With one hand. That's how medical workers learn. They practice giving shots to oranges, and suturing chicken breasts or pigs feet. They do it for 24 hours at a time, until they are so tired they can barely move, until it's an almost automatic response, until they don't even have to think about it anymore.

THE HOSPITAL PECKING ORDER

They may wear tags with the letters MD (for Medical Doctor) after their names, but all doctors are not the same.

INTERNS are new graduates of medical school. They have studied for four years after college and are now ready to start treating patients. For one year they will spend between 60 and 80 hours a week at the hospital.

RESIDENTS have finished interning and spend between two and five years getting more experience. At this point, they will choose an area of medicine, such as emergency medicine or pediatrics, that they want to make a career of.

FELLOWS have spent another three years focusing on a small area in their chosen speciality.

ATTENDINGS are the fellows' and residents' bosses. These doctors have completed their training. But when the problems are very complicated, the attendings might call another doctor in for help.

SPECIALISTS have chosen to focus on one part of the body. There are heart doctors, bone doctors, brain doctors, and more. Every organ of the body has a specialist who is an expert on that part. SUB-SPECIALISTS focus on one area within a specialty, such as newborn babies' heart problems.

A Legacy

For most of human history, there were no ambulances with bright lights to whisk the injured to help…no million-dollar machines…no nurses or doctors waiting to make the hurt go away.
When did all that change?

It's hard to believe that a science devoted to the saving of lives got its start in the bloody trenches of war. But that's just where it happened. In bygone times, a soldier wounded in battle just lay there until a doctor came to the field to treat him. It was usually too late. Until…

BORN ON THE BATTLEFIELDS

In the 1790s the French began to move their wounded soldiers off the battlefields, away from the shooting and the cannons, so they could be safely cared for by doctors and nurses. A simple idea. Just move the victim from the scene to a place where medical care is available. Sound familiar?

Through the years, war continued to tear the world apart. Inventors gave us more powerful weapons…weapons that could inflict more hurts…weapons that left harder-to-treat injuries.

A CROSS OF RED

On June 24, 1859, a Swiss gentleman named JEAN-HENRI DUNANT stumbled upon a scene that would change his life—a battle between Italian and Austrian troops during the Franco-Austrian War. Clouds of smoke filled the sky. Deafening cannon explosions shook the ground. Dunant watched with growing horror. Right there, on the spot, he decided he had to do something. He ran into the nearest village and got the townspeople to help him tend to as many of the victims as he could help.

After he returned home, he got some friends together, and in 1863 the International Committee of the RED CROSS was born. Its workers would wear a white armband so no one would shoot at them. Then, as an honor to the citizens of Switzerland who made it all happen, a red cross was added, making the symbol the opposite of the white cross on a red field that marks Switzerland's flag. That red cross is a symbol of hope and help to this day.

# of Healing

THE WAR BETWEEN THE STATES

A violent civil war tore America apart in the 1860s. One of the true heroes of that dark time was a nurse named CLARA BARTON. She had heard about Dunant's Red Cross and started an American branch of the organization. Compassionate and devoted, she offered aid to the injured of both sides.

As the years passed, wars ended and others started. War and emergency medicine were still tightly linked.

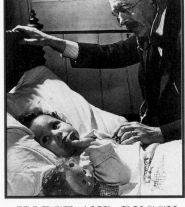

Best foot forward? World War I soldiers set off on a bumpy ride to the hospital. Some ambulances stacked patients six deep.

IS IT A HEARSE OR AN AMBULANCE?

At the turn of the century, the first ambulances started to appear in the larger cities. They simply moved patients to hospital care but did nothing to help along the way. After World War II, ambulance service began to spread to smaller towns and villages. Funeral homes often provided this service, using, as medical transport, the very same cars that carried the coffins to the cemetery. How spooky that must have seemed to someone who was sick! About that time, fire departments began to get involved in moving the injured or ill. Fire stations were staffed 24 hours a day. People got sick 24 hours a day. It all made sense.

BACK TO THE BATTLEFIELDS

During the Korean War, which was fought in the 1950s, MASH UNITS sprang up. MASH stands for MOBILE ARMY SURGICAL HOSPITALS, and they were a major change in the care of the wounded. These portable treatment centers, with operating rooms housed in temporary buildings and even tents, brought first-rate medical care close to the action. Victims could be flown in by helicopter from the battlefields for help. But at home, people who had been injured or who were ill were still only moved to the hospital for care.

THE BIRTH OF THE EMS

The Emergency Medical Service System—well-trained people with lifesaving medical skills working at the scene—got its start in 1966. About the same time, TRAUMA CENTERS, special departments within hospitals, were being created to care for serious medical conditions. The strong chain that links the 911 operators, the EMTs, and the ER team was welded into place.

Today, most hospitals have dedicated emergency medicine departments with a specially trained staff that is used to dealing with the chaos that comes with major trauma. In parts of Europe, helicopters bring a little bit of the hospital right to the accident scene. They can transport an entire sterile operating room, complete with a surgical staff, all in a self-contained unit, directly to the site of a major disaster.

It's been a long, bumpy ride from a crude canvas stretcher, to a horse-drawn coach, to a coffin carrier, to today's sleek ambulances. Along the way, thousands of lives have been saved.

HORSE-AND-BUGGY DOCTORS

What they lacked in knowledge and equipment, they tried to make up with kindness. Just like today's EMTs, America's country doctors of the 1800s braved floods and blizzards to help those in need. They sat with sick children and reassured worried mothers. They set broken bones and bandaged wounds. And they traveled long distances, black medical bag in hand, to sit with someone who needed help. Some things never change.

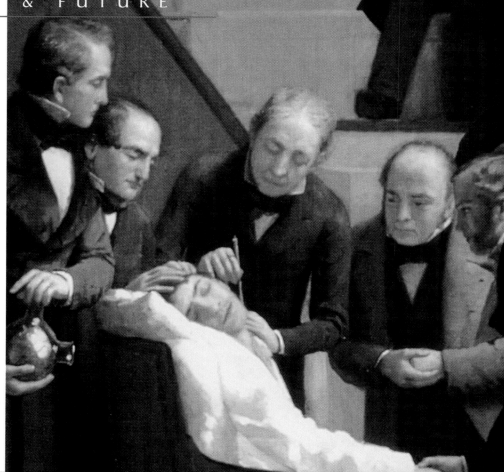

They were men and women who were brave, brilliant, and willing to risk everything to bring hope and good health to millions around the world. Many even experimented on themselves, believing that their discoveries could save lives.

Today, in emergency rooms and operating suites around the world, medical workers depend on these breakthroughs to bring hope to those who need help.

Here are just a few of medicine's greatest moments.

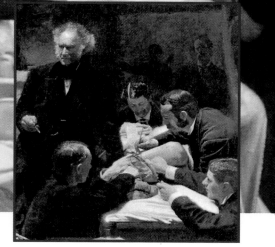

1674. THE MICROSCOPE IS USED IN MEDICINE

Although the first microscopes were invented almost 100 years earlier, ANTONIE VAN LEEUWENHOEK, a Dutchman, built hundreds of microscopes that could magnify over 200 times. He was the first person to see blood cells, bacteria, and the workings of muscles. He described bacteria as "gracefully moving little animals."

1796. THE FIRST INOCULATIONS ARE GIVEN

Nobody likes to get a shot, but it's a lot better than getting really sick. EDWARD JENNER was the first to try fooling the body's immune system into making antibodies to fight viruses. Smallpox was the devastating disease he fought. He made a serum of cowpox, a similar "pox," and injected it into the skin. It worked!

THE 1840s. CLEAN HANDS SAVE LIVES

Hard to believe, but true: Until the 1840s doctors did not wash their hands between patients. Those unwashed hands were spreading disease, not curing it! Surgeons wore the same bloody coat to every operation as a badge of how experienced they were. But a doctor named IGNAZ SEMMELWEIS started the trend toward hand washing when his patients' survival rates soared compared to other doctors'.

Milestones in Medicine

THE 1840s.
SURGERY WITHOUT PAIN

Until this time, surgery was performed without any painkillers. Oftentimes, the pain killed the patient before the operation could be completed! But the discovery of drugs that could put a patient into a deep sleep changed all that.

1881–85. LOUIS PASTEUR BEATS BACK BACTERIA

This great medical mind tackled many problems, giving us a vaccine for rabies (caused by the bite of a diseased animal). But his greatest contribution was an understanding of germs and the damage they do. He developed pasteurization, a heating process that is used to this day to kill germs in milk and juice.

1895. X RAYS REVEAL THE INSIDE TRUTH

While experimenting with light and electrical currents, WILLIAM ROENTGEN accidently stumbled onto an amazing discovery. Working in a dark room with cathode rays, he found that the glowing light bounced off a barium-coated object across the room. When he held his hand up between the light source and the object, he could see every bone in his fingers.

1953. DNA, THE CODE OF LIFE, DISCOVERED

Why do we inherit blue eyes and heart disease? Genes, the instructions that tell our bodies how to work, are made of the chemical dioxyribonucleic acid (DNA). JAMES WATSON and FRANCIS CRICK spent years trying to figure out what DNA looked like. Finally, they did. It's a twisted strand called a double helix. Scientists are now able to find the genes responsible for many chronic illnesses.

What Lies Ahead?

Meet Robo-doc! Experimenting on a happy-to-help skeleton, a team of MDs tries out some new technology—a robot surgeon that can drill the bone for hip replacements with great accuracy.

One hundred years ago, there were no paramedics. No emergency rooms. Few lifesaving surgical techniques. Most people did not survive a serious injury. How times have changed! Now, new treatments are developed every day. The heroic and amazing have become almost routine. But what will the future bring?

Imagine a world where a damaged heart can easily be replaced with an artificial one…a world where a surgeon in New York can operate on a child in France, by remote control. Imagine surgery performed without cutting into the skin. It will all happen—and a lot sooner than we think.

HEART TO HEART

People are sometimes born with defects in certain parts of their bodies—hearts with holes in them, livers or lungs that don't work. Other parts wear out from too much use—knees and hips, for example.

Sometimes surgeons can fix the problem, but many times they can't. The only solution is to find a replacement—a TRANSPLANT of the same organ from another person. But not many spare organs are available. Some patients die waiting.

In the future, artificial parts may be as easy to come by as a spare tire for the car. Artificial replacements are now being used on hips and knees with great success, but eventually almost every part will be replaceable. Doctors are also experimenting with CROSS-SPECIES TRANSPLANTS, especially using pigs. Their genetic makeup is similar enough to ours that they make likely candidates for spare parts.

REMOTE CONTROL

Suppose you live in California but you need a special kind of surgery that can best be performed by a team of doctors in England. Should you get on a plane and fly for 12 hours? Soon you won't have to. Using TV cameras, telephone lines, and computers, those English surgeons will be able to operate by remote control. In fact, certain operations may best be performed by robots like the one shown operating on the skeleton above.

VIRTUAL SURGERY

Do you play a lot of video games? You might make a great surgeon in the future. Since more and more surgery will be done with microscopic cameras and tiny instruments guided into the body by computers, those who can handle a joy stick or computer mouse with ease may find surgery simpler.

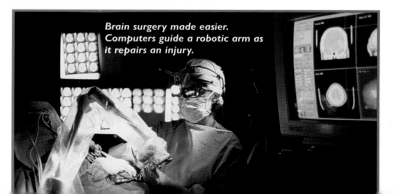
Brain surgery made easier. Computers guide a robotic arm as it repairs an injury.

HOW DOES YOUR BODY GROW?

Scientists have discovered a rare cell in our bodies, found in the bone marrow, that can morph into many different types of tissue. What does that mean? If these cells touch bone, they take on the properties of bone. If they come in contact with cartilage or tendon, they become those things. The good news? Crushed bones and other damaged skeletal parts may soon be rebuilt using this new discovery.

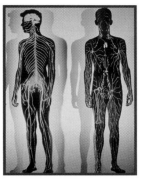

Skin is another thing that is being grown in laboratories. Really bad burns completely destroy all the layers of skin—our bodies' protective covering. Something has to keep all the body fluids from oozing out. Artificial skin works for a couple of weeks, but then the body starts to reject it like an alien invader. But using these cells, scientists can get the patients' skin to regrow with no rejection problems.

USING OUR OWN BODIES TO BATTLE DISEASE

Perhaps in the future, doctors won't need drugs cooked up in the laboratory to fight illness. They are trying to harness the body's own healing defenses to fight back. For example, doctors are experimenting with white blood cells bathed in special proteins that may cure some cancers. And our very genetic makeup may be the key to successfully ending or controlling many terrible diseases. By pinpointing defective genes that cause chronic illnesses, doctors may be able to design "gene bombs" that destroy the renegade cells.

BEAM ME UP

Lasers are used a lot in the operating room nowadays, but other types of rays are paving the way for bloodless, painless surgery in the future. GAMMA-RADIATION KNIVES, which focus tiny beams of cobalt on microscopic brain malformations, can zap tumors without having to cut into the scalp. Beams of ultrasound are being used to speed the healing of broken bones, since doctors have discovered that

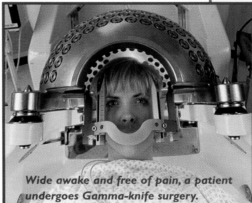

Wide awake and free of pain, a patient undergoes Gamma-knife surgery.

ultrasound stimulates bone-cell formation. Doctors also use a procedure called LITHOTRIPSY, which uses ultrasound waves to "blow up" kidney and gall stones (those are hunks of calcium that form in the body in places other than the bones).

DEFIB TO GO

Every year there are about 14,000 medical emergencies on board American airplanes. Many of those are heart attacks. If a quivering heart is shocked within the first few minutes, the chances for recovery are good. But up in the air, there are no EMTs or ERs. Soon, airplanes may have machines to restart stopped hearts. Defibrillators (see p. 31) may soon be required wherever large groups of people gather, such as planes, trains, and movie theaters. New defibrillators are being designed that are simple enough for a person with no medical background to use. They come with built-in voice commands and sensors that tell whether the patient needs a jolt or not.

NEW "OLD" WAYS TO HEAL

In their search for ways to heal, many doctors are returning to techniques that have been around for centuries. Here are two.

PINS AND NEEDLES

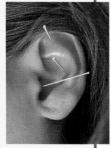

The sight of a body with hundreds of needles sticking out of it might make you shudder, but those needles help stop pain. It's called ACUPUNCTURE and it really works. Many doctors believe that our bodies have a force that flows through them…a river of life. But that river can be blocked, leading to sickness. The pins break down whatever blockages there are. Best of all, the tiny needles can reroute signals of pain so they don't reach the brain. Surgeons now sometimes use acupuncture as an anesthetic for patients whose bodies react badly to sleep-producing drugs.

PARSLEY & SAGE

HERBAL MEDICINE has been around for ages, but its helpfulness is now being reexplored. One-quarter of all prescription medicines come from herbs and other plants. For example, aspirin is made from willow leaves, and St. John's Wort has just been rediscovered as a help for people who are depressed. Now, doctors have found that certain deadly cancers react to plants. For example, a type of periwinkle is used to make a potent leukemia-fighter. Scientists believe that the rain forests still have many undiscovered plants that can save thousands of lives.

10 Things You Can Do Right Now

Medicine is part art, part science, and part good sense. Why not start practicing right now!

1. Start a Family Medical History

For every family member, keep a page in a looseleaf book. Every time someone is sick, jot down the date, what kind of sickness it is, and how long it took to recover. Track colds and sore throats, allergies and tummy upsets. Your information could save a life.

2. Make a Well-Stocked First-Aid Kit

Always have a first-aid box close at hand. The kitchen is an excellent place to keep it. Load it with Band-Aids and antibacterial cream, a roll of gauze and gauze pads, tweezers, a small pair of scissors, a thermometer, safety pins, alcohol wipes, a pair of protective gloves, an Ace bandage, and syrup of ipecac (which makes you throw up and is used in some poisoning cases).

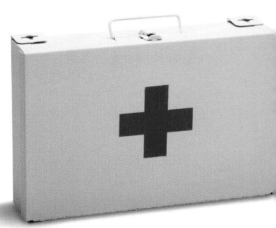

3. Learn How to Use 911

Teach other family members what to do when they dial for help. Remind them to stay on the phone until told to hang up, to speak clearly and to stay calm, and to always do exactly what the dispatcher tells them to do.

4. Remember R I C E

If you or a member of your family sprains an ankle or another joint, here's what to do. REST the affected part. Put ICE on it. Use COMPRESSION by wrapping an Ace bandage firmly around it to reduce swelling. And finally, ELEVATE the affected part.

5. …and B R A T

Upset stomach in the family? Try a BRAT diet to help recover. B is for BANANAS, high in potassium, which helps maintain fluid balances in the body. R is for RICE—plain, boiled, with no butter or salt. A is for APPLESAUCE, gentle on the stomach. T is for TOAST made from white bread. But no butter or jelly until that tummy is feeling better.

6. Be a Helmet-Head

Don't even think of getting on your bike, skateboard, or in-line skates without a safety helmet. Make sure you wear it properly. And if you don't think it's cool to wear one, ask yourself if it's cool to be brain-damaged. And don't forget those wrist guards. The number one in-line skate and skateboard injury ia a broken wrist. Pain is never fun.

7. Make Your Home a Safer Place

Keep a fire extinguisher in your kitchen and learn how to use it. Don't wait until a fire starts to read the instructions. Keep poisons such as cleaning supplies in cabinets where little children can't reach them, and keep the poison control number near the phone.

8. Clean Up Your Medicine Cabinet

Tell your parents to throw out any old prescription medicines. Never save unused portions of antibiotics. Keep prescription drugs locked safely in a dry place—not the bathroom, since moisture from showers and tubs can make them less effective.

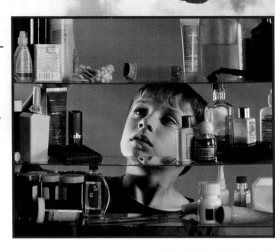

9. Always Wear Your Seat Belt

The best news on the ER scene was the arrival of safety-belt laws and the invention of air bags. The number of messy trauma cases from car accidents has been drastically cut. Some of that improvement is from air bags, but they don't work without seat belts, so always buckle up even if you're just going around the corner.

10. Get Smart

Sign up for an American Red Cross basic first-aid class. Many schools offer classes in the evening. Then when there's an emergency, you'll be ready.

American Red Cross

This certifies that

Joy Masoff

has completed the requirements for

COMMUNITY CPR

WESTCHESTER C

sponsored by

SEP   Date co

Young EMTs and Hospital Helpers

When you are 14 years old, you can help out at your local hospital or volunteer ambulance corps. Hospital volunteers might bring books and magazines to patients. Junior ambulance corps members help bring equipment to the EMTs and clean and stock the rigs, always learning as they go.

IS A LIFE IN MEDICINE FOR YOU?

Do you like helping others? Are you fascinated when an ambulance goes screaming by? You might have the makings of a fine EMT, nurse, or doctor. Why not stop by at your local ambulance corps and ask for a tour? Many will be more than happy to show you the ropes.

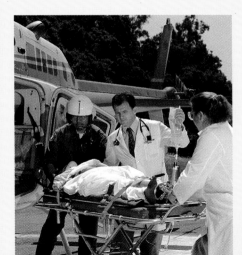

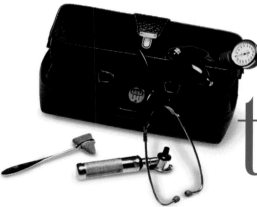

If You'd Like to Learn More

MAGAZINES AND BOOKS

Reading the same magazines the EMTs read offers an exciting glimpse of their world. Here are three good ones.

JEMS: JOURNAL OF EMERGENCY
MEDICAL SERVICES
P.O. Box 469010
Escondido, CA 92046

EMERGENCY
21061 S. Western Avenue
Torrance, CA 90501

RESCUE
P.O. Box 2789
Carlsbad, CA 92018

These books offer additional views of the world of medicine.

KIDS TO THE RESCUE!
First-Aid Techniques for Kids
by Maribeth Boelts and Darwin Boelts
Parenting Press, 1992

MEDICAL TECHNOLOGY:
INVENTING THE INSTRUMENTS
by Robert Mulcahy
The Oliver Press, Inc, 1997

JUST WHAT THE DOCTOR ORDERED:
THE HISTORY OF AMERICAN MEDICINE
Brandon M. Miller
The Lerner Publishing Group, 1996

WHERE TO WRITE

Many worldwide relief agencies depend on help from people just like you. Here are some that you can contact for more information:

AMERICAN RED CROSS
811 Gatehouse Rd.
Falls Chich, VA 22042
This wonderful organization offers basic first-aid and CPR classes all over the country. Write for the location nearest you.

DOCTORS WITHOUT BORDERS
11 East 26th Street
Suite 1904
New York, NY 10010

UNICEF
3 United Nations Plaza
New York, NY 10017

PROJECT HOPE
International Headquarters
Health Sciences Education Center
Carter Hall
Millwood, VA 22646

AMERICAN COLLEGE OF
EMERGENCY PHYSICIANS
P.O. Box 619911
Dallas, TX 75261

WHAT TO WATCH

Most movies and TV shows don't really tell it like it is. This comes the closest.

RESCUE 911 offers up re-creations of thrilling rescues. Check your local TV listings for times.

ONLINE RESOURCES

Excellent Websites exist for the medical field. Try:

http://www.district.north-van.bc.ca/eswsl/www-911.htm
This site will link you to about 2,000 different EMT, fire, medical, and rescue sites. If you click on the button marked EMS, you'll be linked to 600 sites!

AMBULANCE!, an Australian site, is especially interesting. If you like, you can go directly to it at :
http://www.ozemail.com.au/~ddutton/

Another cool site is:
http://www.kidshealth.org/kid/
Take their virtual reality tour of the organs of the body.

For an in-depth look at the workings of the Red Cross try:
http://www.redcross.org/
The history segments are full of wonderful information.

PHOTO CREDITS

Cover: Pete Saloutos/The Stock Market

Endpapers: Brian Michaud

Page 1: Photodisc

Page 2-3: Leo de Wys

Page 4-5: top left and bottom center, Corel; Top right, Peter Escobedo; middle right, Digital Stock; bottom right, Westlight

Page 6-7: Left center, Digital Stock; bottom right, The Stock Market

Page 8-9: top left, Peter Escobedo; far bottom left, Photo Researchers, near bottom left, Digital Stock; center, Peter Escobedo; bottom right' Tony Stone

Page10-11: Top left, top right, Digital Stock; bottom left, Tony Stone; all others, Peter Escobedo

Page 12-13: Top left, Horton Emergency Vehicles; bottom left, Iron Duck; top right, KME; all rescue rig pictures, Barry Smith; all other pictures, Brian Michaud

Page14-15: Top and bottom left, Peter Escobedo; center, Barry Smith; bottom center, Digital Stock, top right, Firehouse; bottom right, Leo De Wys

Page 16-17: Top, Pete Saloutos/The Stock Market; center left and right, Digital Stock; bottom right, Phototake

Page 18-19: All pictures, Brian Michaud, except; bottom left Medichrome; bottom right, Custom Medical Stock; top right, Photodisc

Page 20-21: Left, Phototake; bottom left, Peter Arnold; center (from left to right), Brian Michaud, Washington Stock, Photo Researchers, Washington Stock; top right, Digital Stock; bottom right; Corbis

Page 22-23: All photos Digital Stock, except; bottom left, Phototake; and top right panel, Brian Michaud

Page 24-25: All pictures Photodisc, except, bottom left, middle top, Brian Michaud

Page 26-27: All pictures Digital Stock, except; bottom left, Photo Researchers; center, Custom Medical Stock

Page 28-29: All surgical tools, Brian Michaud; top center, Pete Saloutos/The Stock Market; all others, Digital Stock

Pge 30-31: All photos, Digital Stock except; bottom left, Corel; center right, The Stock Market

Page 32-33: Top left, Corbis; center left, Peter Arnold; bottom left, Peter Freed; center right, Corbis, bottom right, Project Hope, Top right, Doctors Without Borders

Page 34-35: Top left, Westlight; center left, Photodisc; center right, Frank Marchese; top right, Tom Page; center far right, Peter Escobedo, bottom right, Digital Stock

Page 36-37: Bottom left,bottom center and top right, MPI; center top, Simulaids; middle right, Boston Medical Library, far right, Digital Stock

Page 38-39: All pictures, Corbis; except Clara Barton; Digital Stock; ambulance, Ralph La Plant

Page 40-41: Top center, left center, Boston Medical Library; bottom left, Corbis; bottom middle left, Corbis; right center, Corbis, right middle center, Digital Stock far right bottom, Photodisc; top right, all Corbis, except Jonas Salk, MSA

Page 42-43: Top left; George Steinmetz; far left bottom, Peter Arnold; center left, Corbis; right, all Photodisc, except center right, Corbis

Page 44-45: Top left, Brian Michaud; top right, bottom right, Digital Stock; all others Photodisc

THE AUTHOR ALSO WISHES TO THANK:

Nancy Laemle, Director of Public Relations at Northern Westchester Medical Center.

Medical Plastics Incorporated, makers of medical training devices.

A NOTE FROM THE AUTHOR

For the past seven years, I have been a Scout leader, lucky enough to have worked with both Cub Scouts and Girl Scouts. My time with them has been time happily spent. As I shared the opportunities of our world with them, a door was opened to *me*... a chance to see firsthand all the good around me.

Our Boy Scout troop was sponsored by the Golden's Bridge Fire Department, and I was touched by their dedication. Their friendship inspired me to write *FIRE!*, the companion volume to this book.

But I discovered that putting out fires was only a tiny portion of their job. Rescue work and emergency medical care were a huge percentage of their calls.

I began to explore the workings of the Emergency Medical Service and Med-Evac helicopters. That led me into the hospital emergency and operating rooms. I was touched by every single person's intense devotion.

I was lucky enough to be able to scrub up with a surgical team, be strapped into a rescue chopper, and allowed to spend many hours as an observer in the ER. I was given a glimpse of a very special group of people...dedicated, determined, and willing to take great risks to help those in need.

I can only imagine what it must be like to save someone's life. I hope the readers of this book are inspired enough to someday find out for themselves.

A SPECIAL WORD OF THANKS

So many people opened doors, patiently explained things, and allowed me to become a part of their lives. Thank you for your time and help.

Dr. Paul David Kandel of the Mount Kisco (NY) Medical Group

Dr. Barry Kastle and the OR staff, and Monica Gibbs, RN, and the ER staff at Northern Westchester (NY) Medical Center

Karen Barber and Carl Nuebacker of the Lewisboro (NY) Volunteer Ambulance Corps

Barry Smith of the Santa Clara (CA) Fire Department

Dr. Catherine Small and Dr. Hillary Kruger of Montefiore (NY) Hospital

Georgia Relyea of the Phoenix (AZ) Memorial Hospital

The team at Statflight, Westchester (NY) Medical Center

Dr. Frank Avila of the Sterling (Nashville, TN) Medical Group

Peter Pascucchi of the Ossining (NY) Rescue Squad

Thanks also to our expert readers, Dr. Michael W. Shannon of Boston Children's Hospital, Millie Le Blanc, RN, of Good Samaritan Medical Center, Brockton, Massachusetts, and Bill Brown of the National Registry of Emergency Medical Technicians.

And last but never least, with abundant love to my husband and children, Lou, Alex, and Tish Scolnik.